Zoom In on Simple Machines

Wedges

Andrea Rivera

abdopublishing.com

Published by Abdo Zoom™, PO Box 398166, Minneapolis, Minnesota 55439. Copyright © 2017 by Abdo Consulting Group, Inc. International copyrights reserved in all countries. No part of this book may be reproduced in any form without written permission from the publisher. Abdo Zoom™ is a trademark and logo of Abdo Consulting Group, Inc.

Printed in the United States of America, North Mankato, Minnesota
102016
012017

 THIS BOOK CONTAINS RECYCLED MATERIALS

Cover Photo: Rob Cruse/iStockphoto
Interior Photos: Rob Cruse/iStockphoto, 1; Daniela Pelazza/Shutterstock Images, 4; Shutterstock Images, 5, 10, 18, 21; iStockphoto, 6, 8, 9, 16, 19; Designua/Shutterstock Images, 11; Malera Paso/iStockphoto, 12–13; Wang Wen/Imaginechina/AP Images, 14

Editor: Brienna Rossiter
Series Designer: Madeline Berger
Art Direction: Dorothy Toth

Publisher's Cataloging-in-Publication Data
Names: Rivera, Andrea, author.
Title: Wedges / by Andrea Rivera.
Description: Minneapolis, MN : Abdo Zoom, 2017. | Series: Simple machines | Includes bibliographical references and index.
Identifiers: LCCN 2016949162 | ISBN 9781680799569 (lib. bdg.) | ISBN 9781624025426 (ebook) | ISBN 9781624025983 (Read-to-me ebook)
Subjects: LCSH: Wedges--Juvenile literature.
Classification: DDC 621.8--dc23
LC record available at http://lccn.loc.gov/2016949162

Table of Contents

Wedges are **simple machines**.
They can divide objects.

They can cut
them, too.

A wedge is usually made up of two **inclined planes**. They join together to make a sharp edge.

Axes are wedges.
They can split logs.

Downward **force** pushes the ax into the log.

The wedge creates outward force.

This splits the log in two. The ax gives a **mechanical advantage**. Less force is needed to make the split.

Force

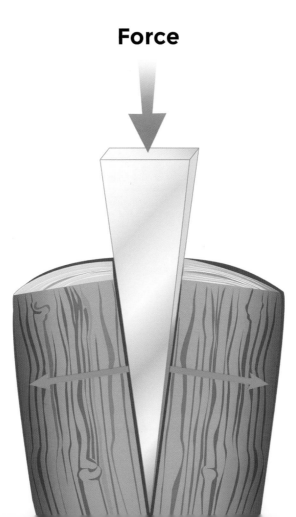

Engineering

A wedge can slice through air. A fan's blades are narrow wedges. A motor inside the fan turns the blades. The blades move air around. This makes the air feel cooler.

Art

Chinese paper cutting uses a wedge.

Artists use a small knife.
It makes tiny slices in paper.
Parts of the paper are cut away.
A picture is left behind.

A wedge is shaped
like a triangle.
It has three sides.

A wedge's **angle** can be different sizes. This changes how much force is needed.

A smaller angle needs
less force to split an object.

A larger angle needs more force.

- Knives are wedges with sharp, narrow edges. People push down on knives to cut things.

- A doorstop is a wedge. It has one inclined plane. A person pushes it sideways under a door. This holds the door open.

- Wedges were one of the first tools used by early people. They used wedges to carve trees into boats.

Glossary

angle - a slope or a slant.

force - a push or pull that causes a change in motion.

inclined plane - a simple machine with a flat surface that is raised at one end.

mechanical advantage - the way a simple machine makes work easier.

simple machine - a basic device that makes work easier.

Booklinks

For more information
on **wedges**, please visit
booklinks.abdopublishing.com

 In on STEAM!

Learn even more with the Abdo Zoom
STEAM database. Check out
abdozoom.com for more information.

Index